Tom Hall

When Hearts are Trumps

Tom Hall

When Hearts are Trumps

1st Edition | ISBN: 978-3-75236-031-8

Place of Publication: Frankfurt am Main, Germany

Year of Publication: 2020

Outlook Verlag GmbH, Germany.

When Hearts are Trumps

By

Tom Hall

The Perfect Face.

The Graces, on a summer day,
Grew serious for a moment; yea,
They thought in rivalry to trace
The outline of a perfect face.
Each used a rosebud for a brush,
And, while it glowed with sunset's blush,
Each painted on the evening sky,
And each a star used for the eye.
They finished. Each a curtaining cloud
Drew back, and each exclaimed aloud:
"Behold, we three have drawn the same,
From the same model!" Ah, her name?
I know. I saw the pictures grow.
I saw them falter, fade, and go.
I know the model. Oft she lures
My heart. The face, my sweet, was yours.

The Moonlight Sonata.

The notes still float upon the air,
    Just as they did that night.
I see the old piano there,—
    Oh, that again I might!
Her young voice haunts my eager ear;
    Her hair in the candle-light
Still seems an aureole,—a tear
    Is my spectroscope to-night.
I hear her trembling tell me "No,"
    And I know that she answered right
But I throw a kiss to the stars, and though
    She be wed she will dream to-night.

The Kiss

Over the green fields, over the snow,
Something I send thee, something I throw.
No one can guess it; no one can know.
Light as a feather, quick as the eye;
Thin as a sunbeam, deep as the sky;
Worthless, but something a queen could not buy.
Ah, you have caught it, love! How do I know?
Sweet, there are secrets lost ages ago.
Lovers learn all of them. Smile not,—'tis so.

The Bride.

Before her mirror, robed in spotless white,
    She stands and, wondering, looks at her own face,
    Amazed at its new loveliness and grace.
Smiling and blushing at the pretty sight,
So fraught is she with innocent delight,
    She feels the tender thrill of his embrace
    Crushing her lilies into flowery lace;
Then sighs and starts, even as though from fright.
Then fleets before her eyes the happy past;
    She turns from it with petulant disdain,
    And tries to read the future,—but in vain.
Blank are its pages from the first to last.
She hears faint music, smiles, and leaves the room
Just as one rosebud more bursts into bloom.

A Problem.

Give you a problem for your midnight toil,—
One you can study till your hair is white
And never solve and never guess aright,
Although you burn to dregs your midnight oil?
O Sage, I give one that will make you moil.
Just take one weakling little woman's heart.
Prepare your patience, furbish up your art.
How now? Did I not see you then recoil?
Tell me how many times it has known pain;
Tell me what thing will make it feel delight;
Tell me when it is modest, when 'tis vain;
Tell me when it is wrong and when 'tis right:
But tell me this, all other things above,—
Can it feel, Sage, the thing that man calls "Love"?

To Phyllis Reading a Letter.

A smile is curving o'er her creamy cheek,
    Her bosom swells with all a lover's joy,
    When love receives a message that the coy
Young love-god made a strong and true heart speak
From far-off lands; and like a mountain-peak
    That loses in one avalanche its cloy
    Of ice and snow, so doth her breast employ
Its hidden store of blushes; and they wreak
Destruction, as they crush my aching heart,—
    Destruction, wild, relentless, and as sure
As the poor Alpine hamlet's; and no art
    Can hide my agony, no herb can cure
My wound. Her very blush says, "We must part."
    Why was it always my fate to endure?

A Rose from her hair.

She gave me a rose from her hair,

    And she hid her young heart within it.

I could hardly speak from despair,

Till she gave that rose from her hair,

And leaned out over the stair

    With a blush as she stooped to pin it.

She gave me a rose from her hair,

    And she hid her young heart within it.

When I told her my Love.

When I told her my love,
  She was maidenly shy,
And she bit at her glove.
I gave Cupid a shove;
  Yes, I begged him to try,
When I told her my love
What was she thinking of
  As she uttered that sigh
And she bit at her glove?
And pray what does it prove
  That she stopped there to sigh,
When I told her my love
And she bit at her glove?

My Lady, you Blushed.

My lady, you blushed.
    Was my love a surprise?
How quickly they hushed!
A curl of yours brushed
    All else from my eyes.
My lady, you blushed.
You say that I gushed,
    And they all heard my sighs?
How quickly they hushed!
Your roses were crushed;
    N'importe wherefores and whys.
My lady, you blushed.

The American Slave.

Come, muster your pleasantest smile, my dear,
    And put on your prettiest gown.
Forget about Jack for a while, my dear,
    His lordship has just come to town.
He's come here to get him a wife, my dear,
    And you have been put up for sale
With a marvellous income for life, my dear,
    To balance your side of the scale.
His lordship is feeble and old, my dear,—
    What odds? All the sooner he'll die.
And he has a sore need of your gold, my dear:
    See the good you can do if you'll try.
And then a real lady you'll be, my dear,
    Not only by nature but name;
Mamma'll be so proud,—you can see, my dear,
    No one thinks it, as you do, a shame.
So bend your proud head. Are you faint, my dear?
    Keep the tears back, be buoyant and brave.
Keep that pose! Now a portrait we'll paint, my dear,
    To be called "The American Slave."

Sell Her,—That's Right.

Sell her,—that's right! She is young, she is fair;
There's the light of the sun in the coils of her hair.
And her soul is as white as the first flakes of snow
That are falling to-night. 'T is a bargain, a"go"
    Sell her,—that's right!
Sell her,—that's right! For a bag full of gold.
Put her down in your ledger, and label her "Sold"
She's only a beauty with somebody's name,
And the Church for a pittance will wash out the shame.
    Sell her,—that's right!

Time and Place.

Hasten on! The mad moonlight isbeaming

On the hatred and love 'twixt us two;

And it beams on the maid who is dreaming,

And the grave made for me or for you.

Time and place,—love and life in the balance,

Fear and hope in the glance of your eye.

Draw your blade! Forget not we are gallants

Who can laugh at our fate as we die.

On your guard! There'll be blood on the metal

Ere she wakes from her innocentdreams;

There's a long list of kisses to settle,

And some love sighs and death sighs, it seems.

Bare your arm! Strike for life and the maiden!

Take that! You are cautious, I fear

Speed the blow,—'tis with happiness laden

For him who does not remain here

That and that! I am wounded,—it's over

Those kisses were destined for you;

But now she is yours and you love her,

Go tell her that I loved her too

Blood on the Rose.

Is it dew on the rose?

'T is the same that I gave him

Last night when I chose

To warn him and save him;

That he pinned on his breast

With a smile at his danger,

And a smile, not in jest,

That was sweeter and stranger

Here are footprints of foes!

Oh, my heart!—I can feel

It is blood on the rose

And a sliver of steel.

In Old Madrid.

I strolled the streets in quest of any love,
    In old Madrid long centuries ago;
I caught the perfume of a scented glove,
    I saw a sweet face in a portico.
She laughed—then paled. She leaned out; whispered, "Fly!"
    And then I felt the sting of steel, the hiss
Of curses in my ear, and knew that I
    Had forfeited my life—and lost a kiss.

The Duel.

Ten paces—one, two, three, and fire!

Two gallants have their heart's desire.

One of them dies, the other laughs;

The seconds smile, the doctor chaffs.

A woman, smiling, dreams she's wed

To—hush, to the very one that's dead.

The Shroud.

The snow came softly, silently, down
Into the streets of the dark old town;
And lo! by the wind it was swept and piled
On the sleeping form of a beggar-child.
It kissed her cheek, and it filled her hair
With crystals that looked like diamonds there;
And she dreamed that she was a fair young bride
In a pure white dress by her husband's side.
A blush crept over her pale young face,
And her thin lips smiled with a girlish grace;
But the old storm-king made his boast aloud
That his work that night was weaving a shroud.

Love's Return.

Love has come back—ah me, the joy!—

Greater than when Love began

To wound my heart. The jocund boy!

Love has come back a gray-haired man.

His eyes are red with tears of woe,

His cheeks are pale, and his heart is sore;

But Love has come back at last, and, oh!

Love will be faithful evermore.

One Wish.

My thoughts are gliding down thestream,

Ah, faster than the river flows;

And idly in my heart I dream

Of islands where the lotus grows.

I fear not rapids, waterfall,

Or whirlpool leading down to death,

If love but my tired heart enthrall,

And I may sip a woman's breath.

I care not what may be my fate.

Roll on, mad river, to the sea;

Drown all ambition, pride, and hate,—

But leave one woman's love to me.

For Me.

I heard her song,
    Low in the night,
From out her casement steal away,
    Nor thought it wrong
    To steal a sight
Of her—and lo! she knelt to pray.
    I heard her say,
    "Forgive him, Lord;
Such as he seems he cannot be."
    I turned away,
    Myself abhorred.
She prayed—and oh! she prayed for me.

To a Water-color.

Sweet Phyllis, maid of yesterday,
    Come down from out that frame,
And tell me why you looked so gay—
    Likewise your other name.
Had bold Sir Plume confessed his love
    And asked you if you'd wed?
And had he called you "Lovey-dove"?
    And how long are you dead?
Where did you get that wondrous gown,
    Those patches, and that hair?
And how were things in London town
    The last time you were there?
And did you die a maid or wife,
    Your husband lord or knave?
And how did you like this jolly life?
    And how do you like the grave?

The Serenade.

Under my casement, as I pray,
My lover sings my cares away
With many a half-forgotten lay.
He leans against the linden-tree,
And sings old songs of Arcady
That he knows well are loved by me.
Half through the night the sweet strains float
Like wind-blown rose-leaves, note by note,
Over the great wall and the moat,
Up to my window, till they teem
Into my soul, and almost seem
To be there even when I dream.
And his heart trembling beats withbliss
If I but throw him one small kiss
Just as I now throw this, andthis

To the Rose in her hair.

Poor little rose, I pity you—

Sweet as Oporto's wind when fruity—

Tortured an evil hour or two,

Just to adorn a wilful beauty.

I know her well, too well, alas!

(Just watch the fairy as she dances.)

She wears my heart—but let that pass;

It's dead: she killed it with her glances.

Your fate, poor rose, is such as mine,—

To be despised when you are faded;

Yet she's an angel—too divine

To be by you or me upbraided.

Her Reverie.

A lady combed her silken hair.
None but a looking-glass would dare
    To gaze on such a scene.
The blushes thronged her dimpled cheek;
They coursed upon her shoulders, eke,
    And the white neck between.
And she was thinking then, I trow,
Of one who, in a whispered vow
    Beneath the budding elm,
Had told her they would sail their barque
On lakes where pale stars pierced the dark,
    With Cupid at the helm.
Anon, a faint smile pursed her lips
And shook her dainty finger-tips,
    As breezes shake the boughs;
And then a quick, impetuous frown
Came gathering from her ringlets down,
    And perched upon her brows.
Ah, she was thinking then, I ween,
Of me, poor clumsy dunce, who e'en
    Had torn her silken dress.
I waltzed too near her at the ball;
Her beauty dazed me—that was all;
    I felt a dizziness.

To Beauty.

"Oh, Mistress Beauty," said my sigh,
　　"I'd laugh to scorn all other blisses,
If you and I might live and die
　　Together on such fare as kisses.
"Your kirtle would not be of silk,
　　The band around it but torn leather.
I think our wine would be plain milk;
　　I think we'd oft see stormy weather.
"But, oh, there are some things in life
　　Worth more to men than fame or money;
And one of them's a sweet young wife,
　　So pure, so honest, and so bonnie."

Dreaming of You.

My soul feels refreshed, like a rose kissed by dew,
When waking I know I've been dreaming of you.
They thought I was mad. Ah, my sweet, if they knew
That my malady simply was dreaming of you!
I've one wish. 'Tis to sleep all the long ages through
By your side, you my bride, and I dreaming of you.

Please Return.

Now, all you pretty maids in town,

Take heed of my sad plight.

I've lost a kiss; I'll give a crown

To get it back to-night.

I threw it, poet-like, I own,

Up to a silvery star;

I must confess I might have known

I could not throw so far.

But, oh, surprise! It circled round,

And sank as though 't were laden

With love—when almost to the ground

'T was caught by some young maiden.

And that young maid I wish to find.

I've lost a kiss, alack!

It is not hers. She'll not be kind

Unless she give it back.

Almost Dying of Ennui.

What are the charms of the sea?

Oh for an hour of the city!

What are the dull waves to me?

Can they say anything witty?

What do they care for my lips?

Why did I come? It's a pity!

Nothing but water and ships,

And Jack far away in the city.

Oh for one ride in the park,

With Jack humming bars from a ditty;

Kissing me (when it grows dark).

Fy! Oh—heigho, for the city!

Jacks from Jack.

Fresh, fragrant, tempting, balmy, red—
    What fool would send them back?
Why do I wish that I were dead,
    With all these jacks from Jack?
Why do I bite my lips and frown,
    Tear buttons off my sacque,
When, just returning to the town,
    I get these jacks from Jack?
Alas, for pleasure's giddy whirl,
    For summer lost, alack!
He's off to see some other girl;
    That's why mere jacks from Jack.

Hyacinths.

Hyacinths, tenderly sweet,
Is it life that you ask in your prayer?
Ah, I would die at her feet,
If I could be one of you there.
There on her billowy breast,
So near to her innocent heart,
That its beating would lull me torest,
And to dream I should never depart.
Sighing are you for the stars?
Look in the depths of her eyes.
Is there a gem of the Czar's
So much like those gems of the skies?
Is it the dew that you miss?
Hyacinths, hyacinths, wait.
Soon she will give you a kiss.
Oh, how I envy your fate!

In The Waltz.

AN ECHO FROM A SEASIDE HOP.

Light as the waves foaming white on the bar,
We dance to the mandolin, harp, and guitar;
One, two, three, waltzing we glide round the room,—
Would you were bride, and ah, would I were groom!
On all the seashore none fairer than you;
What but adore you could any one do?
Cheeks like the pink of an evening sky,
Eyes that might bid a man laughingly die.
Ears like the shells from the Indian sea,
Teeth like white buds on a young apple-tree,
Throat like a lily bent heavy with dew,
Arms just as white and as lily-like too.
Lips that would tempt—ah! you'll pardon me now,
Being so near them suggests, you'll allow,
That the happiest thing e'er a mortal could do,
Would be to be ever thus waltzing with you.

She Is Mine.

There's a sparkle in her eye
That no millionnaire can buy.
If they think so, let them try—
She's divine.
There's a blush upon her cheek
Like the peach-tree's blossom, eke,
Like red willows by the creek,
Or like wine.
She has roses in her hair.
It was I who put them there.
Really, did I ever dare—
Is she mine?
Or is it all a dream,—
Idle poet's empty theme
Put in words that make it seem
    Superfine?
No; for see upon her hand
There's a little golden band,—
Filigree work, understand,
    Like a vine;
And a perfect solitaire
Fits upon it. The affair
Cost two hundred. I don't care!
    She is mine.

Old Times.

Ah, good old times of belles and beaux,
Of powdered wigs and wondrous hose,
Of stately airs and careful grace,
Look you at our degenerate race.
No more the gallant spends his time
In writing of his love in rhyme;
No more he lives unconscious of
All earthly things save war and love.
We modern men have toils and cares
To streak our pates with whitened hairs,
And have to crowd our love and all
Into one short and weekly call.

Of My Love.

Was ever a moon

In joyous June

As royal, radiant, rare as she,

With her smiling lips,

As she lightly trips

Down through the autumn woods to me?

Never a queen

On her throne, I ween,

Had such a loyal slave as I.

Ready to bear

All her cares, I swear,

Just for a fleeting kiss on the sly.

Oh for the day

We gallop away

To the curate's cottage, Gretna Green;

Side by side,

Groom and bride,

Happy twenty and sweet sixteen!

The Farewell.

Not going abroad? What, to-morrow,
And to stay, goodness knows for how long?
Really, Jack, 'twould appear that dry sorrow
Had done even you, sir, a wrong.
It has? Ha, ha, ha! What a joke, sir!
Is it Mabel or Jenny or Nell?
I'm sure you are wrong,—hold my cloak, sir,—
Am I not an old friend? Come now, tell.
The prince of our set broken-hearted!
What a joke! Who rejected you? Speak!
Did you look like that, Jack, when you parted?
Was that pallor of death on your cheek?
You interest me. Tell me about it;
And let your old chum, sir, console.
Hard hit in the heart. I don't doubt it;
You were made for that sort of a rôle.
Did you bend on your knee, like an actor,
Hardly knowing just where to begin?
Was dear mamma's consent the main factor?
What a fool the poor girl must have been!
Who was she? What!—I?—You were jealous?
O, Jack, who'd have thought such a thing?
You've been certainly not over-zealous.
But kiss me—and where is the ring?

The Last Dance.

AN INCIDENT IN A WINDOW SEAT.

He: Well, how many conquests? I fancy a score

By the flush on your cheeks and your shoulders.

She: A bore!

He: Oh, nonsense; a debutante just out of school

Who can rule with a smile what a king could not rule,

From young Harry, her prince, to myself, her poor fool!

Come, tell me, did Harry propose?

She: What a goose

You would think me to tell you, and then of what use

Could it be?

He: Well, it might give me hope, where before

There was none,—quite a boon from the lips you adore

When you 're hungry for love.

She (coquetting): Or who knows but it might—

He: Yes, it might blot from life every semblance of light

As the clouds blot the moon on a storm-troubled night.

But tell me.

She: He did.

He: And your answer was?

She: No.

He: You mean it, or are you coquetting yet?

She: Oh!

I just told him I cared for another—he smiled.

It was merely to him so much pleasure beguiled

From a girl. Charge it up profit?—loss?—tell me which?

He thinks I am pretty, they say, but, not rich.

He would love me, perhaps, for a season or two,

So I told him that I loved another.

He: And who?

She (archly): Really, must I tell *you?*

He: No—your finger—yes, this!

A solitaire—done! and now quickly!

She (feigning reluctance): One!

He (ecstatically): Kiss.

Why he asked for a Vacation.

"Dear Jack:

It's delightfully gay here,—

Old Paris seemed never so fine,—

And mamma says we're going to stay here,

And papa—well, papa sips his wine

And says nothing. You know him of old, dear.

He's only too happy to rest,—

After making three millions in gold, dear.

He's played out, it must be confessed,—

And I—I'm to wed an old Baron

Three weeks from to-day, in great style

(He's as homely and gaunt as old Charon,

And they say that his past has been vile);

And I've promised to cut you hereafter,—

Small chance, though, we ever shall meet,—

So let's turn our old love into laughter,

And face the thing through. Shall we, sweet?

Can you give me up, Jack, to this *roué*,

Just because we may always be poor?

There's still enough time, dear, *et tu es*

Un brave,—you will come, I am sure.

Put your trunk on the swiftest Cunarder,

And don't give me up, Jack, for—well,

There are things in this world that are harder

Than poverty. Come to me!

NELL."

The Editor's Valentine.

The editor sat in his old arm-chair
(Half his work undone he was well aware),
While the flickering light in the dingy room
Made the usual newspaper office gloom.
Before him news from the North and South,
A long account of a foreign drouth,
A lot of changes in local ads,
The report of a fight between drunken cads,
And odds and ends and smoke and talk,—
A reporter drawing cartoons in chalk
On the dirty wall, while others laughed,
And one wretch whistled, and all of them chaffed.
But the editor leaned far back in his chair;
He ran his hands through his iron-gray hair,
And stole ten minutes from work to write
A valentine to his wife that night.
He thought of metre, he thought of rhyme.
'Twas a race between weary brains and time.
He tried to write as he used to when
His heart was as young as his untried pen.
He started a sonnet, but gave it up.
A rondeau failed for a rhyme to "cup."
And the old clock ticked his time away,
For the editor's mind would go astray.
He thought of the days when they were young,
And all but love to the winds was flung,
He thought of the way she used to wear

Her wayward tresses of golden hair.

He thought of the way she used to blush.

He thought of the way he used to gush.

And a smile and a tear went creeping down

The face that so long had known a frown.

And this is what the editor wrote:

No poem—merely a little note,

Simple and manly, but tender, too;

Three little words—they were, "I love you."

Acting.

Ah, my arms hold you fast! How can they be so bold
When my hands offer nothing of silver or gold?
Can it be that I see a new light in your eye?
Can it be that I heard then a womanly sigh?
Ah, I feel such delight, and such joy, such surprise,
That I hardly dare lift my own sight to your eyes
Ah, my arms hold you fast, and my lips touch your cheek,
And I'm crying, "Love, answer me; speak to me—speak!"
And the answer you give to my longing distress
Is that word, with a blush and a kiss, that word "Yes."
Ah, my arms hold you fast, and I burn with a fire
That nothing but long-waiting love can inspire.
Yet I know you mean nothing—mean nothing, because
It's mere acting. Ah me, I can hear the applause.

An Apache Love-Song.[1]

A-atana she was here.

A-atana I was dear.

She will never come again.

Chill my heart, O wind and rain.

A-atana she was here.

Hark, the wind asks "Hi-you?"

And I answer "A-coo,

Ustey with your bitter cold;

U-ga-sha, my love of old."

Still the wind asks "Hi-you?"

"Hi-you?" I know not where.

A-oo, I hardly care.

Take it to the land of snow;

Take it where the stars all go.

"Hi-you?" I do not care.

It-sau-i did it all—

It-sau-i, proud and tall.

Tell her I have gone to fight.

Ask her if her heart is light.

It-sau-i did it all.

[1]

A-atana, yesterday. *Hi-you*, where. *A-coo*, here. *U's-tey*, come, or bring. *U'-ga-sha*, go, or take. *A-oo*, yes. I have no authority for the spelling of these words. I rendered them phonetically from the pronunciation of a young Apache whom I hired to teach me the language. Many Apache words have no perceptible accent. A, here, has the sound of a in father.

The Old-fashioned Girl.

There's an old-fashioned girl in an old fashioned street,
Dressed in old-fashioned clothes from her head to her feet;
And she spends all her time in the old-fashioned way
Of caring for poor people's children all day.
She never has been to cotillon or ball,
And she knows not the styles of the Spring or the Fall;
Two hundred a year will suffice for her needs,
And an old-fashioned Bible is all that she reads.
And she has an old-fashioned heart that is true
To a fellow who died in an old coat of blue,
With its buttons all brass,—who is waiting above
For the woman who loved him with old-fashioned love.

A Retrospect.

I was poor as a beggar,—she knew it,—
    But proud as a king through it all;
Though it cost me two dollars to do it,
    I took little Meg to the ball.
Mere calico served her for satin;
    My broadcloth was made of blue jeans.
Without crest or a motto in Latin,
    Meg's style was as grand as a queen's.
And we were in dreamland all through it,
    And I do not regret it at all;
Though it cost me two dollars to do it,
    I took little Meg to the ball.

Hard Hit.

I guess that I'm done for, old chappie!

Done, whether she loves me or not,—

But don't look so deuced unhappy,—

Y'know it was I fired the shot.

Thanks, awfully. Give me the whiskey,—

There's a horrible pain in my head;

It's queer that my nerves should be frisky

When my heart is as heavy as lead.

I'm worthless; I own it! She told me,

That night at the Country Club ball,—

Don't try, dear old fellow, to hold me,—

Ah, Nellie!—it's over!—don't call!

She told me my life had been wasted,

That my money had ruined my mind,

That I'd not left a pleasure untasted,—

Had been a disgrace to mankind!

And now she's to marry another,—

A poor man, but honest and strong,

Who had never a passion to smother,

And never a chance to do wrong.

He loves her. They'll all think it funny

I don't curse him and kill him, old fel;

But she loves him. I've left him my money,—

For I love her—God bless her! Farewell!

Rejected.

Aw, yes, bah Jove. I thought you'd answer "No."

But still a fellah 's got to awsk, you see.

And then there was the chance you might outgrow

That way you had of making fun of me.

Three years in Europe sometimes make a change

In girls like you, who've always been adored;

And when you laughed, I thought it rawther strange.

Aw, I beg pawdon; p'haps you feel, aw—bored.

You don't? You think it fun—a fellah's pains

At words like yours? You don't know how they smart.

I know you think I haven't any brains;

But still, Miss Nellie, I've a—I've a heart.

Jokers

Her Yachting Cap.

Oh, the little yachting cap
That is lying in her lap
Has a sort of fascination for poor me.
It is made of something white,
And she wears it day and night,
Through the weeks she spends each summer by the sea.
She can make of it a fan,
And, when necessary, can
Hide her face behind it, if she chance to blush.
It has carried caramels,
Chocolate drops, and pretty shells,
And I've even seen her use it as a brush.
But still it has one fault
In my eyes. I'd better halt,
Had I not, and ponder well what I shall say?
She is darting warning glances.
Well, under certain circumstances,
The visor's always getting in my way.

Theft.

The moonlight steals around the pine;

Star-eyes steal radiance from thine.

Low music steals upon the ear;

Can there be theft when thou art near?

I steel my heart for fear of this,—

I steel my heart and steal a kiss.

I'd steal the sacramental wine

If it were sweet as kiss of thine!

Before her Mirror.

I pause before her mirror and reflect
 (That's what the mirror does, I take it, too);
Reflect how little it has known neglect,
 And think, "O mirror, would that I were you."
She has no secrets that you do not know,
 You and yon crescent box of poudre de rose.
And even these long curling irons can show
 Much evidence of use, yet naught disclose.
Here, when she smiles, *you* know it is her teeth
 She's putting to the test ere she depart
For the gay revel on the lawn beneath,
 Or moonlight ramble that may break a heart.
Here she may blush, until she, red as wine,
 Knows that her triumphs have not ceased to be.
Here, when she frowns, and looks still more divine,
 You know, wise mirror, that she thinks of me.

At Old Point Comfort.

You don't think of dresses, or ducats, or dukes;
You don't care for chaperone's rigid rebukes;
    It's just simply grand,
    To lie there on the sand,
        Down at the beach,—
        If a man's within reach.
Some like the moonlight and some like the sun,
Some flirt in earnest and some flirt in fun;
    It's worth all the rash,
    Reckless spending of cash,
    All the dresses you spoil,
    All the tempers you roil,
        Down at the beach,—
        If a man's within reach.
It's better than sleigh-rides, cotillons, or teas,
It makes the dull Patriarch's knickerbocked knees
    Shake in the dance,
    And then one has a chance,
    If one's pretty and smart,
    With a tongue not too tart,
    Of presenting papaw
    With a new son-in-law,
        Down at the beach,—
        If a man's within reach.

A Drop Too Much.

I praised her hair, I praised her lips,
    She looked up with surprise;
I bowed to kiss her finger-tips,
    And then she dropped her eyes.
I said love ruled the world; that I
    Adored her; called her "Nan."
She merely looked a little shy,
    And then she dropped her fan.
I took the hint, and at her feet
    I knelt—yes, quite absurd;
But oh, my fond heart wildly beat
    To hear her drop a word.
I told her all: my talents few,
    My direful lack of pelf.
(We all have erred.) She said "Adieu,"
    And then dropped me myself.

Ingratitude.

Last night young Cupid lost his way,
　　And came to me to find it.
He'd been a truant all the day,
　　But didn't seem to mind it.
I put him in a hansom then
　　For home, and feed the cabby;
But my reward was what most men
　　Would call extremely shabby.
He got his bow and arrows out,
　　And pierced my heart, nor tarried,
But drove away ere I could shout,
　　"Great Heavens, Cupe, I'm married!"

A Few Resolutions.

(*With Reservations*)

He shall never know that I love him—
    Until he asks if I do.
And I'll feel very much above him—
    When he stoops to tie my shoe.
And I shall never kiss him—
    Until he kisses me.
And I shall never miss him—
    Till he sails over the sea.
And I shall never wed him,
    Nor call myself his bride—
Till Cupid and I have led him
    Right up to the minister's side.

A Dilemma.

A letter for me,

From the girl that I love!

Just penned by her hand

And caressed by her glove.

A jewel—a gem—ah!

A letter from Emma.

A letter for me,

Oh, what joy, what surprise!

Just kissed by her lips—

At least, blest by her eyes.

'T is opened—ahem, ah!

A letter from Emma.

A letter for me,

From my sweet little bird.

Eight pages, by Jove!

And I can't read a word.

A precious dilemma,

This letter from Emma!

A Choice not Necessary.

Here is a rose,
Here is a kiss;
Which do you choose?
One rhymes with prose;
One rhymes with bliss.
Ah, you amuse.
You hesitate,
You blush, you sigh.
What! are you loath?
'Tis getting late;
Be quick—
Fool, take them both!

That Boston Girl.

Her voice is sweet,

  Her style is neat;

She'd move the world with but a pen.

  Her mind is clear;

  Her sight, though near,

Is long enough to capture men.

What matters it her learning, then?

The Hero.

He looked so handsome, proud, and brave,
    As he stood there, straight and tall,
With his steadfast eyes, so gray, so grave,
    The beau of the Hunt Club ball.
Ah me, full many a white breast sighed
    For the favor of his hand,—
For the love of a heart so true, so tried,
    For life, you understand.
He looked a hero; he was more,
    A martyr, too, perchance;
For he went to the oldest girl on the floor,
    And led her out to dance.

The Sweet Summer Girl.

She has hair that is fluffy, straight, banged, or half curled;
Has a parasol, oft by her deft fingers twirled.
She has eyes either brown or black, gray or true blue;
Has a neat fitting glove and a still neater shoe.
She has cheeks that make bitter the envious rose;
She has trunks upon trunks of the costliest clothes;
She has jewels that shine as the stars do at night;
And she dances as Ariel dances—or might.
She knows nothing much, but she's great on the smile;
Her profession is love, and she flirts all the while;
She's accustomed to sitting on rocks in the glen;
She is also accustomed to sitting on men.

Her Fan.

Adainty thing of silk and lace,

Of feathers, and of paint,

Held often to her laughing face

When I assume the saint.

Too dainty far to mix with these

Old pipes, cigars, and books

Of bachelordom,—rare life of ease,—

Rare friends, rare wines, rare cooks.

'Twill smell of stale tobacco smoke

Ere many days I fear,

And hear full many a rattling joke,

And feel, perhaps, a tear.

Why is it here? Alas for me!

I broke it at a ball.

"Apologize—repair it" See?

Five dollars gone,—that's all.

Certainty.

Phyllis, love may be for you,

    But it is not for me;

For fortune comes between us two,

    And says it must not be.

Another fellow's fortune, too;

    A million, as I know.

You ask me how I found it out?

    Your mater told me so.

Caught.

When Phyllis turned her eyes on me

I blushed and hesitated;

For though on terms familiar, we

Were not at all related.

I felt her mild, reproachful glance,

And knew her words would rankle.

To tell the truth, I had, by chance,

Been looking at her ankle.

An Important Distinction.

She said, without a single sigh,
    And hardly hesitation,
That she would be my sister, aye,
    Or any fond relation.
I answered cunningly, "Ah me,
    I've sisters by the dozen;
Please make it in the next degree,
    For one may wed a cousin."

Two Kinds.

Oh, her eyes, her beautiful eyes!

How they melt when she sobs or she sighs!

  How they droop

    When she blushes!

  How they flash

    When she crushes

The love she's compelled to disguise!

Oh, her i's, her beautiful i's!

Who can tell them apart though he tries

  From her m's

    Or her e's,

  N's, or u's

    As you please

  In her letters? I offer a prize.

What it Is.

Just a little melancholy,
    Just a tear or two,
Just a word that's naughty,
    Just a spiteful "pooh!"
Just an extra cocktail,
    Just a flower-bill due,
Just another ring to take
    Unto my friend, the Jew.
That is what it is to be
    Rejected, Miss, by you.

In her Pew.

She looked up from her pew

(Why she did, Heaven knows);

But I smiled; wouldn't you?

'T was the right thing to do;

And, pshaw, nobody knew.

Then I tried hard to pose,

But a look of hers froze

All my blood. And I woo

Her in future, old chappie, when not in her pew.

The Suspicious Lover to the Star.

O silver star,
That seeth far,
Tell my poor heart what she is doing;
And ease my pain,
Who would again
Be at her side, and still be wooing.
Does she regret
The token set
By me upon her slender finger?
Or in the dance
Do her eyes glance
At it sometimes,—and sometimes linger?
Be, silver star,
Particular,
And do not be afraid of hurting.
I know her well,
And truth to tell,
I fear my lady love is flirting.

A Slight Surprise.

Come, lovely Laura! strike the lyre,

  And I will sing a song to thee

That will thy maiden heart inspire

  With love, and love alone for me.

Why hesitate? Come, strike the lyre!

  Down where the chord is minor D.

Of wooing thee I'll never tire.

  Good gracious! Why do you strike me?

Past vs. Present.

Through all the days I courted her
    My memory fondly floats,
When love and I exhorted her
    To read, re-read my notes.
But now I love her ten times more,
    And my soul fairly gloats
To think that my hard times are o'er,—
    For now she pays my notes.

The Usual Way.

Three young maidens sat in a row,

With three grim dragons behind ‘em;

And each of these maidens had a young beau,

And they all of ‘em made ‘em mind ‘em.

These three maidens are married now;

In three brown-stone fronts you’ll find ‘em.

But ever since the very first row

They can none of ‘em make ‘em mind ‘em.

A Difference in Style.

Sweet Phyllis sat upon a stile,
    With love and me beside her,
Her red lips in a pouting smile.
    A pout? Her eyes belied her.
My thoughts were merry as the day,—
    And though the joke was shocking,—
I shouted quick, and turned away:
    "A spider's on your stocking!"
The fun, of course, I did not see,
    But heard an exclamation
That sounded much like "Gracious me!"
    And guessed the consternation.
Then Phyllis sat upon the style
    Of men who would deride her;
But she no longer sits the while
    With love and me beside her.

Afraid.

Down the broad stairs,
    Stranger to cares,
My love comes tripping and smiling and free;
    The snows on her breast
    Are a blush unconfessed.
I wonder what fate has in waiting for me?
    My heart seems to throb
    Like a broken-paced cob;
I fear I'm a coward in love, as they say.
    She's commencing to laugh;
    How the fellows will chaff.
By Jove, I'm not going to ask her to-day.

Ye Retort Exasperating.

"Sweete maide," ye lovesicke youthe remarked,
"Thou'rt fickle as my star!
By far ye worste I ever sparked,
You are! You really are!
Albeit yt my brains are nil,
I'm gallante as can be;
I'lle be to you whate'er you wille,
If you'lle be more to me."
"Faire youthe," ye maide replied, "I do
Not barter, as a rule,
But I'lle be sister untoe you,—
Be you my Aprille foole."

A Rhyming Reverie.

It was a dainty lady's glove;

A souvenir to rhyme with love.

It was the memory of a kiss,

So called to make it rhyme with bliss.

There was a month at Mt. Desert,

Synonymous and rhymes with flirt.

A pretty girl and lots of style,

Which rhymes with happy for a while.

There came a rival old and bold,

To make him rhyme with gold and sold.

A broken heart there had to be.

Alas, the rhyme just fitted me.

A Sure Winner.

Oh, treat me not with cold disdain,
    My pretty maids of fashion;
Look upon the hearts you've slain,
    And listen to my passion.
Though I am not so peerly proud
    As men of higher station,
So handsome that the madding crowd
    Collects in admiration;
And have, perhaps, too great a store
    Of sandy hair and freckles,
I've mortgages and bonds galore,
    And muchly many shekels.
You yet may journey league or mile
    To wed, as you're aware.
Come, cease your longing for mere style,
    And take A. MILLIONNAIRE.

Tantalization.

She stands beneath the mistletoe
    As though she did not know it.
She looks quite unconcerned, you know,
    And pretty, yes,—but, blow it,
I have to turn and walk away;
    I'll have revenge anon.
She knows quite well, alack the day,
    That my wife is looking on.

His Usual Fate.

All one season
    Lost to reason,
Breathing sea air
By the beach, where
    Young hearts mingle,
Love was playful
All the day full.
    We were single.
Now with mournful
Looks and scornful
Turns he too us;
He is through us,
    Worried, harried.
Love is sighing;
Love is dying.
    We are married.

On Two Letters from Her.

I wrote her a letter. It took her quite two
    To answer it after she'd read it.
My letter contained what perhaps even you
    Have written,—at least, you have said it.
My letter contained the old tale of a heart
    That longed to be linked to another;
And I told her to think on each separate part,
    And ask the advice of her mother.
She apparently did, for the very next mail
    Brought me a message of woe.
It took her two letters; they made me turn pale;
    For they were the letters "N" "O".

A Serenade—en Deux Langues.

Sous le maple, mort de night,

Avec le lune beams shining through,

Ecoutez-moi, mon hapless plight.

Je vous aime—qui lovez-vous?

Je plink les strings de mon guitar.

Il fait bien froid; J'am nervous, too.

Dites-moi, dites-moi ce que vous are?

Je vous aime; qui lovez-vous?

Tu es si belle, je veux vous wed.

Mon père est riche—comme riche est you?

Bonne nuit, adieu; J'ai cold in head.

Je vous aime—qui lovez-vous.

When a Girl says "No."

When a girl says "Yes,"
There's a quick caress,
A kiss, a sigh,
A melting eye.
There's a vision of things
That hard cash brings,—
A winter at Nice
With a servant apiece,
A long yachting cruise,
Name in "personal news,"
Plenty of wine,
Two hours to dine;
But it's different quite when a girl says "No."
When a girl says "No,"
It's so different, oh!
No kiss, ten sighs,
Two tear-dimmed eyes.
There's a vision of things
That poverty brings,—
A winter complete
On Uneasy Street,
A temptation to rob,
A twelve-dollar job,
A boarding-house meal,
And you pray a new deal;
For it's different quite when a girl says "No."

Uncertainty.

Jenny has a laughing eye,

Yet she is most wondrous shy.

But why?

Jenny says she hates the men;

Still she'll marry. Artful Jen!

But when?

I've a rival who is rich;

With one of us sweet Jen will hitch.

But which?

Her Peculiarities.

The Question of the Learned Man.

How doth the little blushing maid
    Employ each shining hour?
Doth she, in sober thought arrayed,
    Learn knowledge that is power?
Say, doth she mend her father's socks,
    And cook his evening meal?
And doth she make her own sweetfrocks
    With adolescent zeal?

The Reply of the Observant Youth.

Not much; not much. She knows it all;
    She doth not need to learn.
She thinks of naught but rout or ball,
    And which youth will be her'n.
She hustles for a diamond ring;
    She cares not for her dad.
She does not make him anything,—
    Except, she makes him mad.

Tying the Strings of her Shoe.

Tying the strings of her shoe,

    With only the moon to see me.

Could I be quick? Could you?

That is the time to woo

What would any one do?

    I tied no knot that would free me,

Tying the strings of her shoe,

    With only the moon to see me.

When You are Rejected.

Don't say

    "Good day,"

Then grab the door and slam it.

    Be quite

    Polite;

Go out, and then say, "– it."

A Bachelor's Views.

A pipe, a book,
A cosy nook,
A fire,—at least its embers;
A dog, a glass;—
'T is thus we pass
Such hours as one remembers.
Who'd wish to wed?
Poor Cupid's dead
These thousand years, I wager.
The modern maid
Is but a jade,
Not worth the time to cage her.
In silken gown
To "take" the town
Her first and last ambition.
What good is she
To you or me
Who have but a "position"?
So let us drink
To her,—but think
Of him who has to keep her;
And *sans* a wife
Let's spend our life
In bachelordom,—it's cheaper.

My Cigarette.

Ma pauvre petite,
My little sweet,
    Why do you cry?
Why this small tear,
So pure and clear,
    In each blue eye?
'My cigarette—
I'm smoking yet?'
    (I'll be discreet.)
I toss it, see,
Away from me
    Into the street.
You see I do
All things for you.
    Come, let us sup.
(But oh, what joy
To be that boy
    Who picked it up.)

Discovered.

AN EPISODE ON BEACON HILL.

You are frowning;

I don't wonder.

Reading Browning;

Hard as thunder!

Oh, excuse me;

You adore it?

You amuse me;

I abhor it.

Let me see it.

Who has taught you?

Now to me it—

Ah, I've caught you.

It *must* be hard so

(Hence the frown?)

To read the bard so—

Upside down.

The Ice in the Punch.

The wail of the 'cello is soft, sweet, and low;
There are strains of romance in the thrumming banjo.
The violin's note—feel it float in your ear;
And the harp makes one fancy that angels are near.
The voice of a young girl can reach to the heart;
The song of the baritone—well, it is art.
The flute and the lute in gavotte—the guitar
In soft serenade—how entrancing they are!
    But to all the mad millions
    Who dance at cotillons
There's naught like the clink and the clank and the crunch
    Of the ice in the punch.
So here's to the recipe, ancient in Spain,
And here's to the basket of cobwebbedchampagne.
Again to the genius who grows the sharp spice,
But ten times to King Winter who furnishes ice;
    For to all the mad millions
    Who dance at cotillons
There's naught like the clink and the clank and the crunch
    Of the ice in the punch.

The Tale of a Broken Heart.

She was a
    Beautiful,
    Dutiful,
        Grand,
And rollicking queen of Bohemia,
    With a cheek that was
        Rosier,
        Cosier,
                And
As soft as a lily, and creamier.
    She was always com-
        pelling me,
        Selling me,
                I
Was her slave, but she treated me shamefully.
    She went on the
        Stage, was a
        Rage, as a—
                Why—
As a page, and they spoke of her blamefully.
    And then in the
        Papers her
        Capers were
                Writ.
I love her no longer,—I swearit;
    But I oft spend a
        Dollar and

Holler and

Sit

Through her antics. Oh, how can I bear it?

Where did you get it?

Pray, ladies, ye of wondrous clothes,
That draw admiring "ahs!" and "ohs!"
And "By Joves!" as men chat,
Permit me,—love the right bestows,—
Where did you get that hat?
The very hat, sweet maids, I mean,
So often now on Broadway seen,
That is so very flat;
Black as a rule, but sometimes green.
Where did you get that hat?
In shape an oyster-dish,—the crown,—
A ribbon bristles up and down,
Quite striking—yes, all that;
The sweetest, neatest thing in town!
Where *did* you get that hat?

No

"No!" The word
Fell upon my ears
Like the knell of a funeral bell.
I had fondly expected
A whispered "yes" that
Would steal into my soul
Like the song of an angel
From some distant Aidenn.
I arose and brushed off
The knees of my trousers.
"Farewell," I said; "you have ruined my life."
"Nonsense," she replied in the cold, cutting voice
Of a woman who has been used to $100 bills
And a coupé;
"There have been thirty-seven before you, and they
Are all married and happy now.
You see I know all about young men."
"I do not think a young, timid girl
Should 'No' so much," I answered. And going out
(Carefully escorted by the butler, for there was
A better overcoat than mine in the hall),
I left her alone and unloved,—with no one to care for her
Save a couple of dozen servants
And a doting father and mother.

A Midsummer Night's Tempest.

AN EPILOGUE TO HAMLET, PERFORMED BY AMATEURS.

SCENE: *Elsinore—a platform before the castle (on an improvised stage). Inky darkness. Shade of Hamlet (solus).*

Shade of Hamlet: Oh, did you see him, did you see the knave,

The spindle-shanked, low-browed, and cock-eyed

Clerk to an attorney, play at Hamlet,

Dream-souled Hamlet, wearing an eyeglass?

Oh, it was horrible.

(*Enter Shade of Laertes.*)

Shade of Laertes: What's the matter with Hamlet?

S. of H.: He's not all right.

No, by the fame of Shakespeare, he's allwrong.

A certain convocation of talented amateurs

Are e'en at him.

Your amateur is your only emperor for talent;

There's not a genius in the universe

Who will essay as much.

S. of L.: Or, who will imitate nature so abominably.

Your head is level, Ham., and I—even I,

Laertes, suffered at the hands of one

Whose fiery hair, parted in the middle

Like a cranberry pie, caused me to believe

That some of nature's journeymen had made a man,

And not made him well, he imitated nature

So abominably.

S. of H.: Ha' the fair Ophelia!

(Enter Shade of Ophelia.)

S. of O.: Yes, my lord, thine own Ophelia,
Come back to earth with heaviness o' grief
Thy madness ne'er begot, for I have seen
The efforts of a lisping, smirking maid,
As graceful as a bean-pole, and as lean.
Attempt to paint the sorrow of myheart.
Oh, I would get me to a nunnery.
S of H.: Let me Ophelyour pulse.
Mad—quite mad; and all because
A creature whom these mortals call a Miss,
Quite properly, as her efforts are amiss,
Would fain portray thee. Soft you, now!
O fair Ophelia. Nymph in thine orisons
Be all her sins remembered.
Why let the stricken deer go weep,
The untrained amateur play?
All those that watch must surely weep.
So wise men stay away.
(*Flickering blue lights and curtain.*)

The Abused Gallant.

Two lovely maidens (woe is me!)
    Play tennis with my heart;
And each is wondrous fair to see,
    And each is wondrous smart.
In learning, money, beauty, birth,
    None can surpass them—none.
But each receives my "court" with mirth,
    And tells the other one.
My "court"! The term is fitly used—
    A tennis court, you see.
And I know well I am abused,
    By the "racket" they give me.
Maud strikes my heart a brutal blow,
    And Mabel cries out, "Fault!"
And back and forth I undergo
    A feminine assault.
Maud asks my age. Alas! I hear
    Sweet Mabel say, "The goose
Is very nearly forty, dear."
    Maud answers, "Oh, 'the deuce'!"
And so my poor heart with their wit
    Is volleyed oft and oft,
Till Mabel cries, while holding it,
    "This heart is far too soft."
And firing it into the net,
    She says, with girlish vim,
"Although he isn't in our 'set,'

We're making 'game' of him."
And making game they are, I swear
By all the saints above,
With all the terms of tennis there
Save but the sweetest, "love."

After the Ball.

A last word in the vestibule,
    A touch of taper fingers,
A scent of roses, sweet and cool,
    When she has gone still lingers.
He pauses at the carriage door
    To sigh a bit and ponder
He thinks the matter o'er and o'er,
    And all his senses wander.
With mantle thrown aside in haste,
    Her heart a bit uncertain,
And neither time nor love to waste,
    She watches through the curtain.
And she has played him well, he knows
    Nor has he dared to stop her.
She wonders when he will propose;
    He wonders how he'll drop her.

Vanity Fair.

Oh, whence, oh, where

Is Vanity Fair?

I want to be seen with the somebodies there.

I've money and beauty and college-bred brains;

Though my 'scutcheon's not spotless, who'll mind a few stains?

To caper I wish in the chorus of style,

And wed an aristocrat after a while

So please tell me truly, and please tell me fair,

Just how many miles it's from Madison Square.

It's here, it's there,

Is Vanity Fair.

It's not like a labyrinth, not like a lair.

It's North and it's South, and it's East and it's West;

You can see it, oh, anywhere, quite at its best.

Dame Fashion is queen, Ready Money is king,

You can join it, provided you don't know athing.

It's miles over here, and it's miles over there;

And it's not seven inches from MadisonSquare.

For the Long Voyage.

"Were I a captain bold," I said,
    And gently clasped her hand,
"Wouldst sail with me, by fancy led,
    To every foreign strand?
"Wouldst help me furl my silver sail,
    And be my trusty crew?
Wouldst stand by in the midnight gale,
    My pilot tried and true?"
"Well, no," she answered, blushing red,
    "Such heavy work I hate.
But,"—listen what the maiden said,—
    "I would be your first mate."

This is the end.